I0425865

Assessment of Benthic Macroinvertebrate Communities at Cape Lookout and Cape Hatteras National Seashores, 2010

Natural Resource Data Series NPS/SECN/NRDS—2011/395

Joseph C. DeVivo and M. Brian Gregory

National Park Service
Southeast Coast Inventory and Monitoring Network
625 Phoenix Road
Athens, GA 30605

October 2012

U.S. Department of the Interior
National Park Service
Natural Resource Stewardship and Science
Fort Collins, Colorado

The National Park Service, Natural Resource Stewardship and Science office in Fort Collins, Colorado publishes a range of reports that address natural resource topics of interest and applicability to a broad audience in the National Park Service and others in natural resource management, including scientists, conservation and environmental constituencies, and the public.

The Natural Resource Data Series is intended for the timely release of basic data sets and data summaries. Care has been taken to assure accuracy of raw data values, but a thorough analysis and interpretation of the data has not been completed. Consequently, the initial analyses of data in this report are provisional and subject to change.

All manuscripts in the series receive the appropriate level of peer review to ensure that the information is scientifically credible, technically accurate, appropriately written for the intended audience, and designed and published in a professional manner.

Data in this report were collected and analyzed using methods based on established, peer-reviewed protocols and were analyzed and interpreted within the guidelines of the protocols.

Views, statements, findings, conclusions, recommendations, and data in this report do not necessarily reflect views and policies of the National Park Service, U.S. Department of the Interior. Mention of trade names or commercial products does not constitute endorsement or recommendation for use by the U.S. Government.

This report is available from the Southeast Coast Network (http://science.nature.nps.gov/im/units/secn) and the Natural Resource Publications Management website (http://www.nature.nps.gov/publications/nrpm/)

Please cite this publication as:

DeVivo, J. C. and M. B. Gregory. 2011. Assessment of benthic macroinvertebrate communities at Cape Lookout and Cape Hatteras National Seashores, 2010. Natural Resource Data Series NPS/SECN/NRDS—2011/395. National Park Service, Fort Collins, Colorado.

NPS 603/117342, October 2012

Contents

Summary and Key Findings

In July 2010, the Southeast Coast Network (SECN) Inventory and Monitoring Program in cooperation with the University of Georgia Marine Extension Service (MAREX) conducted an assessment of water and sediment quality at Cape Lookout and Cape Hatteras National Seashores as a part of the Network's Vital Signs Monitoring program (DeVivo et al. 2008, Gregory et al. *in review*). The sampling occurred during the Deepwater Horizon Oil Spill in the time period when the scientific community was uncertain as to whether the oil and dispersant plume would enter the Gulf Stream and potentially affect coastal systems along the South Atlantic Coast. In an effort to acquire as much baseline data as possible, the SECN collected benthic marine invertebrate samples following the EPA National Coastal Assessment (NCA) protocols at sites where water and sediment chemistry assessments were conducted. Estuarine benthic communities can be good indicators of ecological condition and environmental stressors because of their limited mobility, occurrence in habitats where contaminant and hypoxia stress are potentially elevated, and because they are sources of nutrients and energy (and potential pathway for contaminants) to other organisms (USEPA 1995).

The purpose of this document is to report the data collected for the macroinvertebrate community at Cape Lookout and Cape Hatteras National Seashores using the EPA Southeast Coast Benthic Index (Van Dolah et al. 1999), which provides a measure of benthic health. This report has been designed to provide data to resource managers in a concise summary format, and in the context of applicable federal standards that were developed by the U.S. EPA. Other data collected during this survey are available at (http://www.nature.nps.gov/publications/NRPM).

1. Sediments were collected following the methods as outlined in the 2010 National Coastal Condition Assessment Field Operations Manual using a Young-modified Van Veen Grab sampler. Sediment samples were filtered through a 0.5mm mesh, non-living items such as rocks and sticks were removed, and the remaining filtrate was preserved for taxonomic identification.

2. Species were identified to the lowest practical level following NCA lab and quality control protocols.

3. Across all sites, 5,583 individuals in 148 taxa were identified, with gem clam (*Gemma gemma*) accounting for 3,740 (67%) of all individuals observed. Only four species were found in at least half of the samples: seed shrimps (Ostracoda, 14 sites), the polychaete *Leitoscoloplos fragilis* (13 sites), channeled barrel-bubble (*Acteocina canaliculata*, 13 sites) and gem clam (nine sites).

4. Using the criteria set forth in the Southeast Coast Benthic Index, overall benthic conditions in both brackish and saltwater systems were *Good* (healthy benthos), with only 2 of 22 sites receiving overall ratings of *Fair* (some stress).

Introduction

Estuaries are semi-enclosed coastal bodies of water that have free connection with the open sea and within which sea water mixes with fresh water. A defining feature of an estuary is that it is an interface between seawater and fresh water and there is an influence of the ocean tide creating a dynamic relationship between the two waters. Estuaries contain critical habitat for a variety of fish and wildlife species. They serve as nursery habitats for fish, crustaceans, and shellfish and foraging habitat for birds and mammals. Additionally, they provide a multitude of recreational opportunities including boating, fishing, and bird watching. These are fragile ecosystems vulnerable to impacts caused by development and many other uses. Urban and industrial development has been shown to negatively impact estuaries severely by altering hydrodynamic processes, increasing exposure to levels of chemical contaminants that cause mortality, altered growth, and reduced reproduction of aquatic life, and increased exposure to more frequent and severe hypoxia (Lerberg et al. 2000). When nutrients from various sources, such as sewage and fertilizers, are introduced into an estuary, the concentration of available nutrients will increase beyond natural background levels. This unnatural increase in organic matter may result in a host of undesirable water-quality conditions. Excess nutrients can lead to increased chlorophyll, which can decrease water-clarity and lower concentrations of dissolved oxygen. In addition, macrobenthic communities in impacted areas are often characterized by low diversity, low numbers of rare and pollution sensitive species, and low abundances (Lerberg et al. 2000). In areas with increased impervious cover, stormwater runoff is flashier and occurs in greater volumes than in undeveloped areas. This unnatural runoff can often be polluted with a wide variety of low-level contaminants that are released into estuaries and can accumulate in sediment (Holland et al. 2004).

A wide variety of metals and organic substances, such as polycyclic aromatic hydrocarbons (PAHs), polychlorinated biphenyls (PCBs), and pesticides, are discharged into estuaries from urban, agricultural, and industrial sources in the watershed. The contaminants adsorb onto suspended particles and eventually accumulate in depositional basins where they can disrupt the benthic community of invertebrates, shellfish, and crustaceans that live in or on the sediments. To the extent that the contaminants become concentrated in the organisms, they pose a risk to organisms throughout the food web—including humans.

Several factors influence the extent and severity of contamination. Fine-grained, organic-rich sediments are likely to become resuspended and transported to distant locations and are also efficient at scavenging pollutants. Thus, silty sediments high in total organic carbon (TOC) are potential sources of contamination. Conversely, organic-rich particles bind some toxicants so strongly that the threat to organisms can be greatly reduced

Cape Lookout (CALO) and Cape Hatteras (CAHA) National Seashores are adjacently located and separately maintained park units along the Outer Banks of the North Carolina coast stretching from Beaufort Inlet on the south to Bodie Island on the north. Together these parks encompass over 59,000 acres of beaches, upland maritime forests, tidal creeks and salt marshes. Cape Lookout and Cape Hatteras National Seashores share a common geological history and are composed of a chain of transgressive and regressive barrier islands, formed during the Pleistocene glacial period from a large dune ridge which was located east of the Outer Bank's current location. The dune ridge gradually migrated westward during the Holocene as sea levels rose until approximately 4,000 years ago when wind, waves, and currents formed the present configuration of islands. All of these islands are subject to periodic inlet formation, migration, closure, and seawater overwash during severe storms (Mallin et al. 2004).

Purpose and Scope of Study

In July 2010, the Southeast Coast Network (SECN) Inventory and Monitoring Program in cooperation with the University of Georgia Marine Extension Service (MAREX) conducted an assessment of water and sediment quality at CALO and CAHA as a part of the Network's Vital Signs Monitoring program (DeVivo et al. 2008). The sampling occurred during the oil spill in the time period when the scientific community was uncertain as to whether the plume would enter the Gulf Stream and potentially affect coastal systems along the South Atlantic Coast.

Estuarine benthic communities can be useful indicators of ecological condition and environmental stressors because of their limited mobility, occurrence in habitats where contaminant and hypoxia stressors are potentially elevated, taxonomic and functional diversity, and because they are a source of nutrients and energy (and potential pathway for contaminants) to other organisms within the ecosystem (USEPA 1995). In an effort to acquire as much baseline data as possible, the SECN collected benthic marine invertebrate samples following the EPA National Coastal Assessment protocols at a subset of sites where water and sediment chemistry assessments were conducted as a part of the Network's Vital Signs Monitoring Program (see Gregory and Smith [2011] for a summary of water and sediment chemistry findings).

The purpose of this document is to summarize and report the benthic macroinvertebrate community data collected at Cape Lookout and Cape Hatteras National Seashores using the EPA Southeast Coast Benthic Index (Van Dolah et al. 1999), which provides a measure of benthic habitat quality. This report has been designed to provide data to managers in a concise summary format in the context of applicable federal standards that were developed by the U.S. EPA. Other data collected during this survey are available at (http://www.nature.nps.gov/publications/NRPM).

Study Area

Cape Hatteras National Seashore

Cape Hatteras National Seashore is the northern most park unit in the SECN (Figure 1). Located along the northern section of the Outer Banks, Cape Hatteras contains 35,400 acres (14,326 ha) of land and 74 miles (119 km) of virtually unspoiled beaches. The U.S. Fish and Wildlife Service administers Pea Island National Wildlife Refuge within the boundary of the Seashore. Seashore marshes contribute heavily to primary estuarine productivity and provide habitat for numerous wildlife and aquatic species. The unique and varied habitats, such as mature broad-leafed evergreen forest and shrub, freshwater marsh, and bog support an unusual assemblage of aquatic, terrestrial, and avian species. Buxton Woods also overlies, protects, and provides for recharge of an important freshwater aquifer. The Seashore has recently been designated a Globally Important Bird Area by the American Bird Conservancy because of the importance of the Seashore habitats to avian breeding, migration, and wintering.

The ecological zonation of CAHA is due in part from artificial alterations dating from the turn of the 20th century. The most important perturbations were due to (a) early efforts at mosquito control and waterfowl management which involved excavation of drainage ditches and construction of water control structures, and (b) construction and vegetative stabilization of primary dunes along the length of the Seashore. Later changes were wrought when road construction included excavation of borrow ponds for road bed material. For the most part, these actions ended by the 1970s, save for localized projects designed to protect specific and discrete portions of infrastructure.

Nags Head (located on the northern end of the Seashore), as well as nine other smaller towns, border the Seashore causing some developmental pressure from outside the park. Visitor and recreational uses represent the major categories of threat to the integrity of natural resources on the CAHA. Replacement of natural areas with impervious surfaces increases storm-water runoff with its associated contaminants, so it may be of potential concern to offshore water quality. Many areas in the vicinity of the park have water bodies that have recently been 303(d)-listed. Shell fishing has been prohibited in areas to the south of Kill Devil Hills and Manteo due to elevated pathogen levels as well as several smaller areas long the Seashore that have been 303(d) listed.

Cape Lookout National Seashore

Cape Lookout National Seashore, located along the southern end of the Outer Banks, is largely undeveloped and accessible only by boat. Cape Lookout is made up of three barrier islands covering 56 miles (90 km) of the central coast of North Carolina (Figure 2). Most of the Seashore consists of North and South Core Banks, a 44-mile (71 km) long barrier system oriented in a southwest to northeast direction and separated New Drum Inlet. CALO extends into the Atlantic Ocean from its southern end. The other barrier system within the Seashore, Shackelford Banks, extends westward from Cape Lookout.

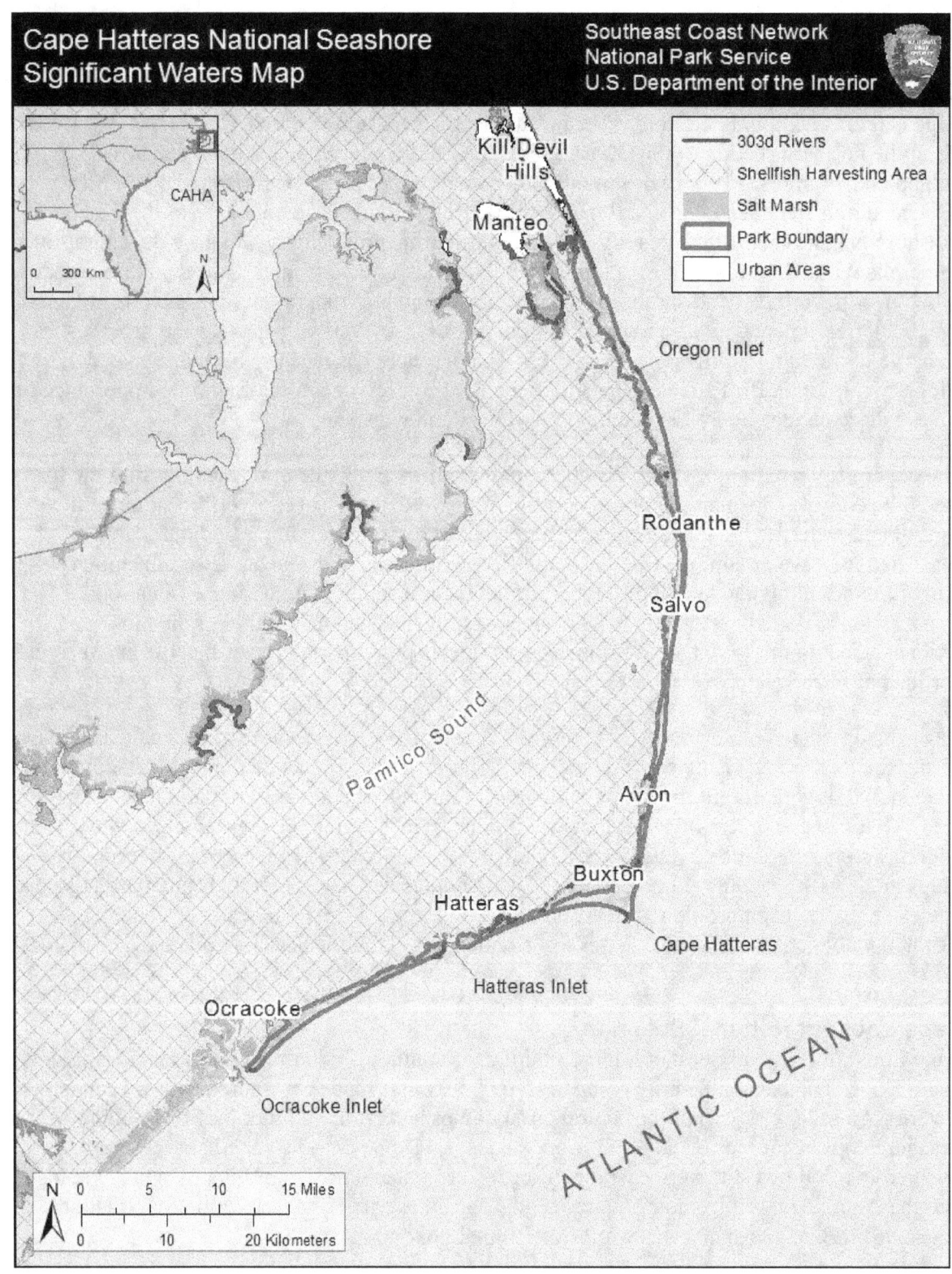

Figure 1. Map showing estuarine and marine water resources in the vicinity of Cape Hatteras National Seashore in North Carolina. Indicated are areas of salt marsh (USFWS 2011), urbanization (US Census Bureau, 2001), 303(d) listed water bodies (USEPA 2011), and areas designated as having special uses or restrictions (NCDENR 2011).

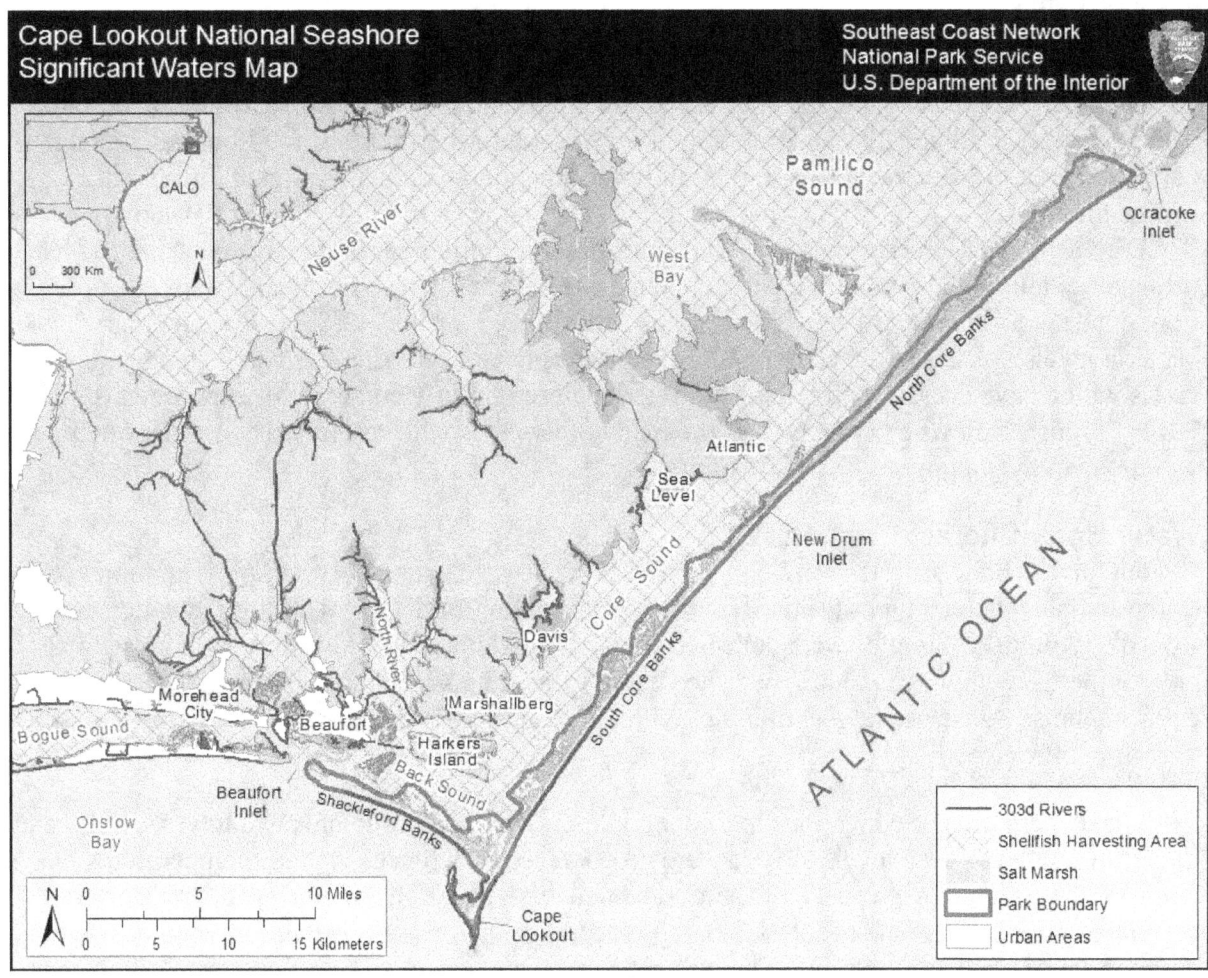

Figure 2. Map showing estuarine and marine water resources in the vicinity of Cape Lookout National Seashore in North Carolina. Indicated are areas of salt marsh (USFWS 2011), urbanization (US Census Bureau 2001), 303(d) listed water bodies (USEPA 2011), and areas designated as having special uses or restrictions (NCDENR 2011).

Core Banks is a long, narrow expanse of low dunes, maritime grasslands, and extensive salt marshes. Shrub thickets border the grassland in many places, and a low maritime forest occupies small areas of higher ground, such as Guthrie's Hammock. The islands are generally about 3–6 feet (0.9–1.8 m) in elevation and 0.6–1.2 miles (1–2 km) in width. For the most part, they are open and treeless.

Instead of exhibiting the typical zonation of a wide berm, low dunes, grasslands and shrub thickets, and salt marsh, the northern end of Portsmouth Island is characterized by vast tidal sand flats (averaging 0.6 miles in width) located between the berm and the dunes in a series of marsh-fringed islands. At triangular-shaped Cape Lookout, continuous dunes similar to those on Shackleford Banks can be found on the southwest side, with several small freshwater marshes present in depressions between the dunes. With high dunes significantly reducing overwash, thickets have further stabilized the flats of the Cape's interior. A long spit extends from the western tip of Cape Lookout, where a jetty built in the early 1900s has encouraged accretion in this direction.

Specific issues of concern to CALO include off-road vehicle use and associated impacts to dunes, threatened and endangered species, commercial fishing, military over flights, and non-native species. Additionally the Back Sound off Shackleford Banks at Cape Lookout drains the populated areas of Morehead City and Beaufort,although no National Pollutant Discharge Elimination System (NPDES) discharges are located on the Core or Shackleford Banks (NCDENR 2001). Numerous water bodies in the vicinity of the Seashore have been 303(d)-listed for water quality violations. For example the marine waters off both north and south of Cape Lookout as well as those off the Cape Lookout itself have been listed for elevated mercury and bacteria levels. Areas in the Core and Bogue Sounds have been listed for elevated pathogen levels which have caused shell fishing areas to be closed or only conditionally approved (USEPA 2011). Figure 2 shows these as well as the many other areas with recently listed water quality violations in the vicinity of Cape Lookout.

Water Body Characterizations

Benthic invertebrate samples were collected at 22 sites within sound (19 samples) and inlet (three samples) habitat types (Table 1). With the exception of the two sampling locations in Roanoke Sound, all samples were collected in polyhaline-euhaline (saltwater or > 18 ppt) environments, with the remaining two sites being located in oligohaline-mesohaline (brackish) environments. All sampling locations are within the northern latitudes (> 35°N) of the EMAP Carolinian Province.

With the exception of the locations in Roanoke Sound, inlet environments had lower salinity and higher dissolved oxygen levels. There were no observed differences in water temperatures among habitats, and the presence of submerged aquatic vegetation and marine debris was not correlated with habitat type (Table 1). Sample depths ranged from less than 0.5 m to nearly 6 m, with the majority of sites (18 of 22) being between 0.5 and 1.5 m.

Table 1. Chemical and physical attributes of locations where benthic marine invertebrate communities were sampled at Cape Lookout and Cape Hatteras National Seashores, 2010 [SAV – Submerged Aquatic Vegetation; DO – Dissolved Oxygen; ● – Present; ○ – Not observed].

Water Body	Site	Depth (m)	SAV	Marine Debris	Temp (°C)	pH	DO (mg/L)	Salinity (ppt)
Roanoke Sound	ALT03	0.51	○	○	28.11	8.32	6.89	13.06
Roanoke Sound	ALT19	1.21	○	○	27.94	8.27	7.38	16.80
Pamlico Sound	02	1.27	○	○	28.38	8.1	5.65	22.66
Pamlico Sound	06	0.80	●	○	27.83	7.89	6.13	21.94
Pamlico Sound	17	3.66	●	○	26.21	7.97	6.62	27.98
Pamlico Sound	21	1.21	●	○	28.16	8.26	6.98	22.93
Pamlico Sound	ALT05	5.79	○	○	26.93	8.13	6.43	27.08
Pamlico Sound	ALT07	1.02	○	○	28.26	8.16	5.52	20.84
Pamlico Sound	ALT12	0.51	●	○	33.51	8.74	9.23	29.58
Pamlico Sound	ALT17	0.97	○	○	31.02	8.32	8.09	27.95
Pamlico Sound	ALT28	1.23	○	○	29.41	8.15	7.09	32.27
Core Sound	08	1.42	○	●	29.13	8.09	6.86	35.68
Core Sound	12	1.02	○	○	28.00	8.33	4.41	35.69
Core Sound	26	0.91	●	○	24.61	7.94	5.15	32.78
Core Sound	ALT06	1.22	○	●	27.02	8.04	6.06	35.34
Core Sound	ALT10	1.35	○	○	27.79	8.26	5.62	35.16
Core Sound / Back sound	20	1.22	●	●	29.49	8.09	6.72	35.55
Back Sound	04	1.07	○	○	29.98	8.15	6.52	35.28
Back Sound	ALT02	4.27	○	○	27.98	8.1	6.76	35.02
Oregon Inlet / Roanoke Sound	01	0.76	●	○	27.47	8.11	6.25	20.34
Hatteras Inlet / Pamlico Sound	10	2.13	○	○	28.62	8.18	5.37	24.29
Hatteras Inlet / Pamlico Sound	ALT27	0.36	●	○	29.53	8.17	5.41	20.6
Sounds								
Min		0.51			24.61	7.89	4.41	13.06
Max		5.79			33.51	8.74	9.23	35.69
Average		1.61			28.41	8.17	6.53	28.61
Standard Deviation		1.39			1.87	0.19	1.07	7.11
Inlets								
Min		0.36			27.47	8.11	5.37	20.34
Max		2.13			29.53	8.18	6.25	24.29
Average		1.08			28.54	8.15	5.68	21.74
Standard Deviation		0.93			1.03	0.04	0.50	2.21

[1] Salinity concentrations less than 18 ppt require separate assessment criteria due to environmental drivers of community composition (Hyland et al, 1998).

Methods

Benthic macroinvertebrate community assessment was conducted in estuarine and tidal creek waters following the methods developed by the Environmental Protection Agency's National Coastal Assessment Program (U.S. EPA 2010). Site selection and sampling methodology are briefly outlined in the following sections.

Site Selection

Thirty sites within the boundaries of Cape Lookout and Cape Hatteras National Seashores were randomly selected for monitoring water quality and sediment contaminants following methods developed by the U.S. EPA (2010). This method of randomly selecting sites in a spatially balanced manner provides managers with a statistically valid estimate of the overall conditions of assessed resources within or around the parks (Stevens 1997, Stevens and Olsen 1999, Stevens and Olsen 2004). Benthic invertebrate samples were collected at a subset of 22 locations where the concurrently sampled water and sediment quality took place, and where site depth and substrate type met the criteria for adequate sampling (Figure 3; Gregory and Smith 2011).

Benthic Invertebrate Sample Collection and Processing

Sediments were collected following the methods as outlined in the 2010 National Coastal Condition Assessment Field Operations Manual (USEPA 2010). A 0.04 m^2, stainless steel, Young-modified Van Veen Grab sampler was used to collect samples for benthic macroinvertebrate analyses at the same time and locations that water and sediment toxicity samples were collected. Sediment samples were filtered through a 0.5 mm mesh, and after rinsing, large non-living items such as rocks and sticks were inspected for organisms and removed. The remaining filtrate was then retained and preserved in a 100% buffered formalin solution for later specimen identification. All sampling equipment was rinsed and cleaned between sampling locations to minimize cross-contamination of samples.

In December 2011, samples were sorted, and all organisms were analyzed by EcoAnalysts, Inc. for species composition and abundance. Species were identified to the lowest practical level following NCCA protocols (USEPA 1995, 2001). Additionally, 20% of each sample was re-sorted by a second taxonomist to ensure a minimum of 90% sorting efficiency and identification accuracy (see Appendix B for results of the QA/QC assessment).

Benthic Community Assessment Criteria

Benthic community condition was measured using the Southeast Coast Benthic Index (Van Dolah et al. 1999), which includes four measures: (1) mean abundance, (2) mean number of taxa, (3) 100 minus percent abundance of the top two numerically dominant taxa, and (4) percent abundance of pollution-sensitive taxa (Table 2). Condition assessments were calculated at the scales of both the sampling location and study area. Scores of 1, 3, or 5 were assigned for each metric and site using the criteria in Table 2. Overall community condition is calculated as the average metric score for each site, which was assigned a condition category of *Good*, *Fair*, or *Poor* using the criteria in Table 3.

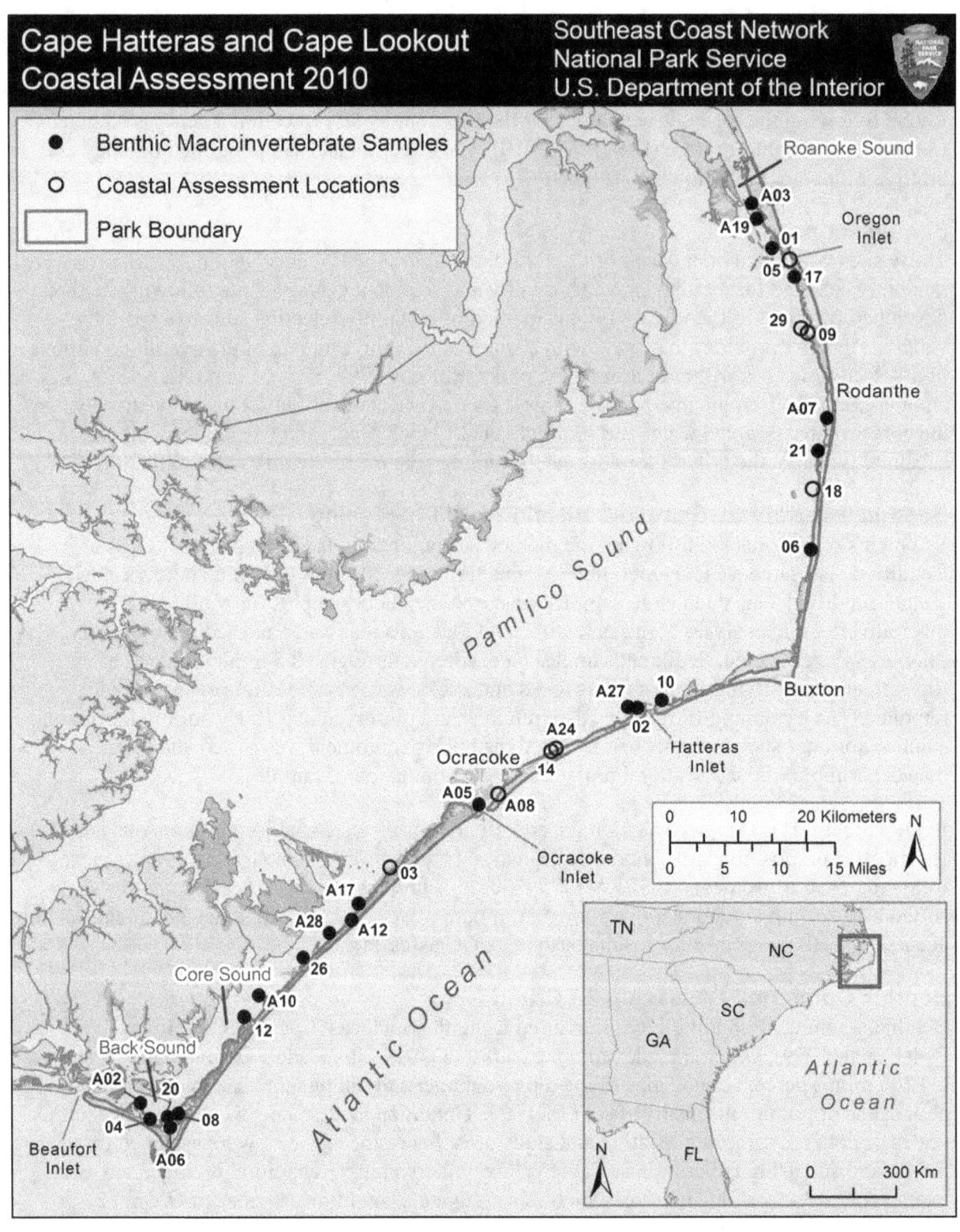

Figure 3. Location map showing sites sampled at Cape Lookout and Cape Hatteras National Seashores during July 2010.

Table 2. Scoring criteria applied to benthic community samples collected at Cape Lookout and Cape Hatteras National Seashores, 2010. Metrics and scoring criteria from the Southeast Coast Benthic Index (modified from Van Dolah et al. 1999).

Component Metric	Oligohaline-mesohaline (brackish) All latitudes			Polyhaline-euhaline (saltwater) Northern latitudes		
	1	3	5	1	3	5
Number of individuals per 0.04 m^2	<53.50	53.50 – 93.00	>93.00	<26.00	26.00 – 109.75	>109.75
Number of taxa per 0.04 m^2	<7.00	7.00 – 8.50	>8.50	<7.5	7.5 – 17.00	>17.00
100 minus % of two most dominant taxa	<9.62	9.62 – 25.45	>25.45	<28.94	28.94 – 51.53	>51.53
% Pollution-sensitive taxa[a]	<0.61	0.61 – 5.04	>5.04	0	0 – 12.83	>12.83

[a] Percentage of individuals within the taxa Ampeliscidae, Haustoriidae, Tellinidae, Lucinidae, Hesionidae, Cirratulidae, *Cyathura polita*, or *Cyathura burbancki*.

Table 3. Condition assessments applied to site- and parkwide-average Southeast Coast Benthic Index scores.

Rating	Index Score	Inferred Site Quality
Good	3.0 – 5.0	Healthy Benthos
Fair	2.0 – 2.5	Some Stress
Poor	1.0 – 1.5	Unhealthy Benthos

Results

Across all sites, 5,583 individuals in 148 taxa were identified, with gem clam (*Gemma gemma*) accounting for 3,740 (67%) of all individuals observed. Only four species were found in at least half of the samples: seed shrimps (Ostracoda, 14 sites), the polychaete *Leitoscoloplos fragilis* (13 sites), channeled barrel-bubble (*Acteocina canaliculata*, 13 sites) and gem clam (nine sites). An average of 18 taxa were found per site across all samples.

Abundance
The number of individuals found at each site ranged from 24 to 2,838, with fewer taxa found on average in the brackish sites than in the saltwater sites (Table 4). Two saltwater sites had abundance values much higher than the other sites, largely due to large numbers of gem clam, which comprised more than 90% of the individuals at those sites. Abundance values were considered to be low for the brackish sites, where the abundance metric received a value of 1 (Table 5), but overall most sites received scores of 3 or 5 (Figure 4). The overall score for the abundance metric in saltwater sampling locations was 5 (Table 5).

Number of Taxa
The number of taxa present at each sampling location ranged from 7 to 45 with the fewest taxa being recorded at the two brackish sites. As a result, the two samples from Roanoke Sound received metric scores of 1, with all other sites except Site A05 scoring 3 or 5 (Table 5, Figure 5). The parkwide score for the number of taxa metric was a 5 (Table 5).

Dominance
Four sites had communities dominated by one or two species, but in general, dominance scores were 3 or 5 (Figure 6, Table 5). Across both parks, average scores were 3 in the saltwater sites and 5 in the brackish water sites.

Sensitive Species
The percentage of individuals considered as sensitive taxa ranged from 0% (at three sites) to 67.5% (Table 4). Although site index scores varied, index scores across the entire study area in both the saltwater and brackish locations were 5 (Table 5, Figure 7).

Overall Benthic Community Condition
Overall benthic conditions in both brackish and saltwater systems are *Good*, with only two sites receiving overall ratings of *Fair*. No discernible spatial patterns of component metric scores were apparent.

Table 4. Values for Southeast Coast Benthic Index metrics for sites sampled at Cape Hatteras and Cape Lookout National Seashores, 2010. Park-wide average scores are presented separately for both polyhaline-euhaline (saltwater) and oligohaline-mesohaline (brackish) sites due to salinity-specific differences in assessment criteria.

Water Body Name	Site	Number of Individuals	Number Of Taxa	Percent Dominance	Percent Sensitive
Roanoke Sound	A03	31	7	35.5	19.4
Roanoke Sound	A19	35	6	34.3	0.0
Pamlico Sound	2	29	8	31.0	6.9
Pamlico Sound	6	83	17	60.2	0.0
Pamlico Sound	17	77	11	36.4	67.5
Pamlico Sound	21	63	17	63.5	0.0
Pamlico Sound	A05	24	7	20.8	16.7
Pamlico Sound	A07	65	18	70.8	15.4
Pamlico Sound	A12	882	14	5.3	0.1
Pamlico Sound	A17	2838	16	1.1	0.5
Pamlico Sound	A28	100	10	20.0	3.0
Core Sound	8	228	45	79.8	8.8
Core Sound	12	140	22	50	10.0
Core Sound	26	81	20	61.7	12.4
Core Sound	A06	64	21	59.4	9.4
Core Sound	A10	42	16	42.9	14.3
Core Sound / Back sound	20	83	18	54.2	13.2
Back Sound	4	114	22	60.5	32.5
Back Sound	A02	91	29	83.5	16.5
Oregon Inlet / Roanoke Sound	1	60	13	50.0	25.0
Hatteras Inlet / Pamlico Sound	10	227	30	38.3	54.6
Hatteras Inlet / Pamlico Sound	A27	176	24	46.0	17.0
Park-Wide Averages					
Polyhaline - Euhaline (saltwater) Sites		273	18.9	46.8	16.2
Oligohaline - Mesohaline (brackish) Sites		33	6.5	34.9	9.7

Table 5. Component scores for Southeast Coast Benthic Index metrics for sites sampled at Cape Hatteras and Cape Lookout National Seashores, 2010. Park-wide average scores are presented separately for both polyhaline-euhaline (saltwater) and oligohaline-mesohaline (brackish) and are based on average metric values for each system as presented in Table 4.

Water Body Name	Site	Number of Individuals	Number Of Taxa	Percent Dominance	Percent Sensitive	Average Score
Roanoke Sound	A03	1	3	5	5	3.5
Roanoke Sound	A19	1	1	5	1	2
Pamlico Sound	2	3	3	3	3	3
Pamlico Sound	6	3	3	5	1	3
Pamlico Sound	17	3	3	3	5	3.5
Pamlico Sound	21	3	3	5	1	3
Pamlico Sound	A05	1	1	1	5	2
Pamlico Sound	A07	3	5	5	5	4.5
Pamlico Sound	A12	5	3	1	3	3
Pamlico Sound	A17	5	3	1	3	3
Pamlico Sound	A28	3	3	1	3	2.5
Core Sound	8	5	5	5	3	4.5
Core Sound	12	5	5	3	3	4
Core Sound	26	3	5	5	3	4
Core Sound	A06	3	5	5	3	4
Core Sound	A10	3	3	3	5	3.5
Core Sound / Back sound	20	3	5	5	5	4.5
Back Sound	4	5	5	5	5	5
Back Sound	A02	3	5	5	5	4.5
Oregon Inlet / Roanoke Sound	1	3	3	3	5	3.5
Hatteras Inlet / Pamlico Sound	10	5	5	3	5	4.5
Hatteras Inlet / Pamlico Sound	A27	5	5	3	5	4.5
Park-Wide Averages						
Polyhaline - Euhaline (saltwater) Sites		5	5	3	5	4.5
Oligohaline - Mesohaline (brackish) Sites		1	1	5	5	3

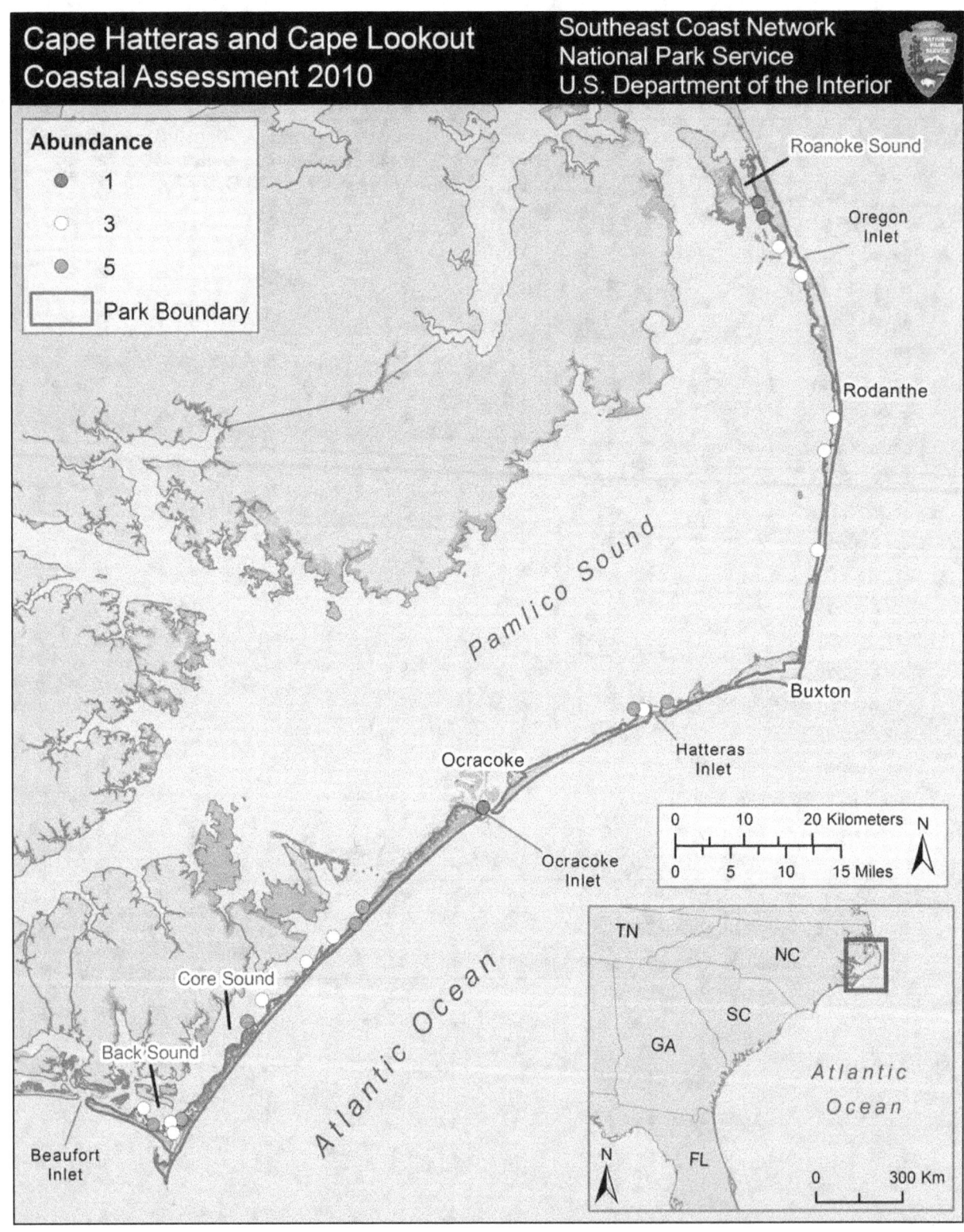

Figure 4. Component scores for the abundance metric of the Southeast Coast Benthic Index based on samples collected at Cape Hatteras and Cape Lookout National Seashores, 2010. Sites were given scores of 1 (*Poor*), 3 (*Fair*), or 5 (*Good*) based on criteria presented in Table 2 (From Van Dolah et al. 1999).

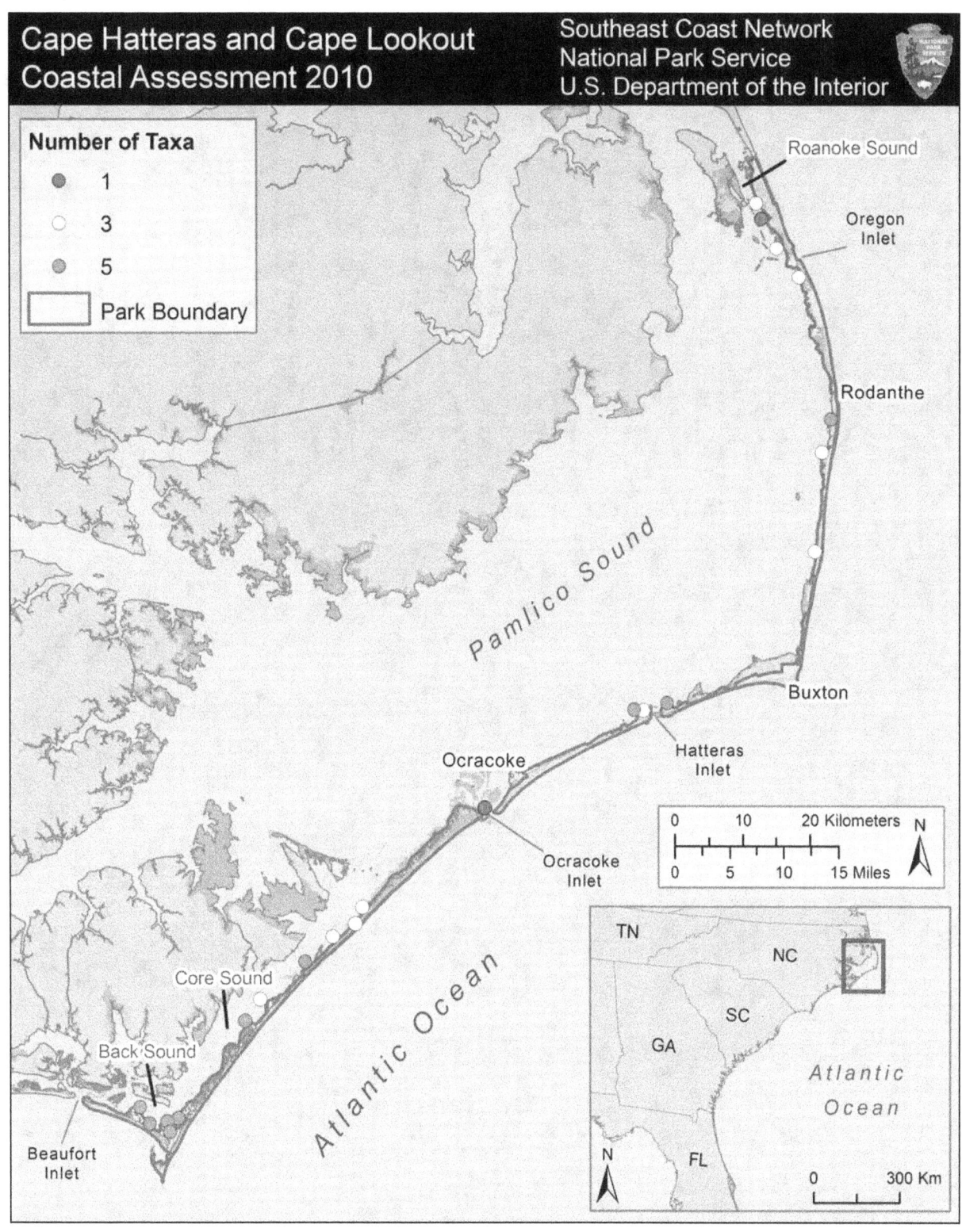

Figure 5. Component scores for the number of taxa metric of the Southeast Coast Benthic Index based on samples collected at Cape Hatteras and Cape Lookout National Seashores, 2010. Sites were given scores of 1 (*Poor*), 3 (*Fair*), or 5 (*Good*) based on criteria presented in Table 2 (From Van Dolah et al. 1999).

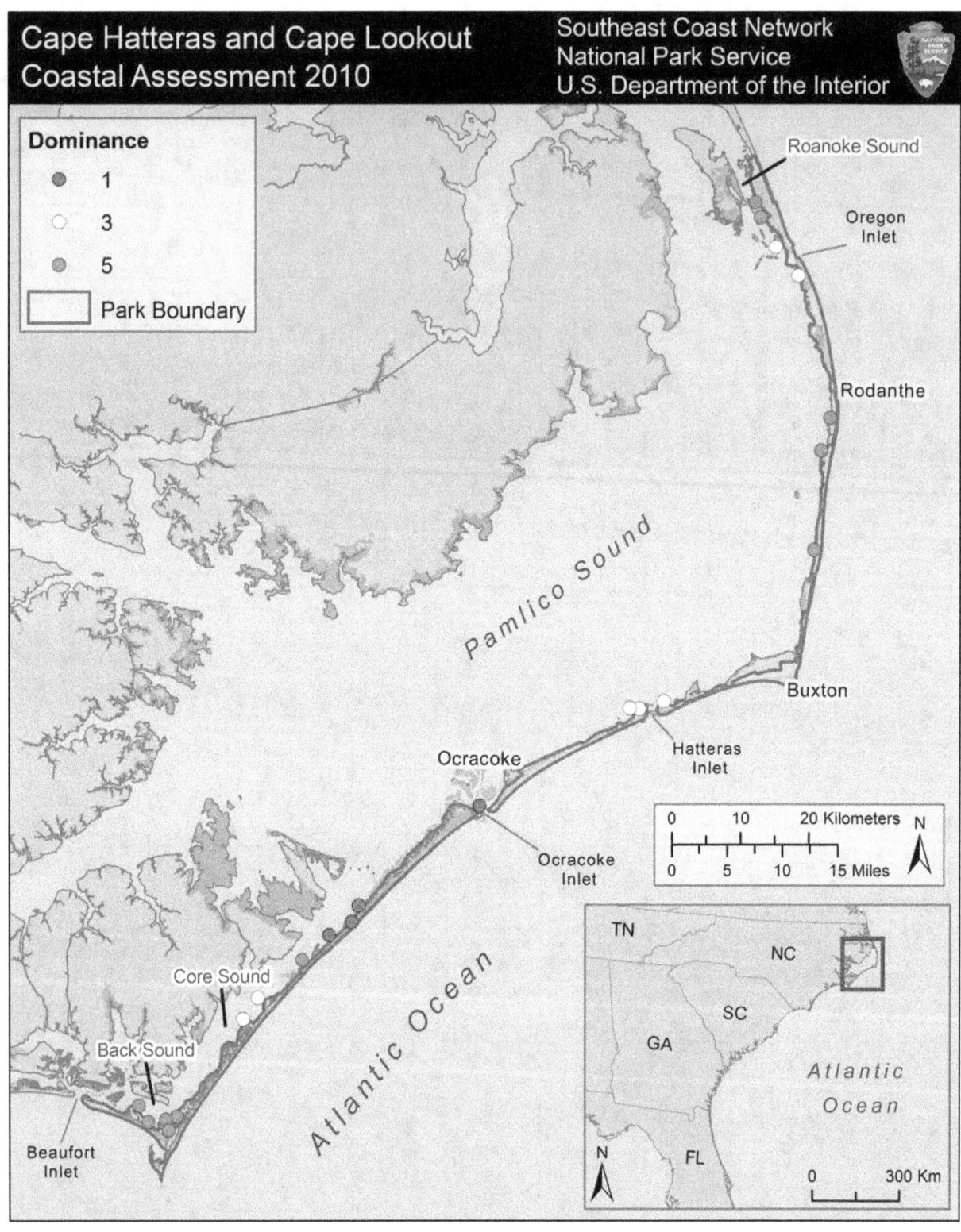

Figure 6. Component scores for the dominance metric of the Southeast Coast Benthic Index based on samples collected at Cape Hatteras and Cape Lookout National Seashores, 2010. Sites were given scores of 1 (*Poor*), 3 (*Fair*), or 5 (*Good*) based on criteria presented in Table 2 (From Van Dolah et al. 1999).

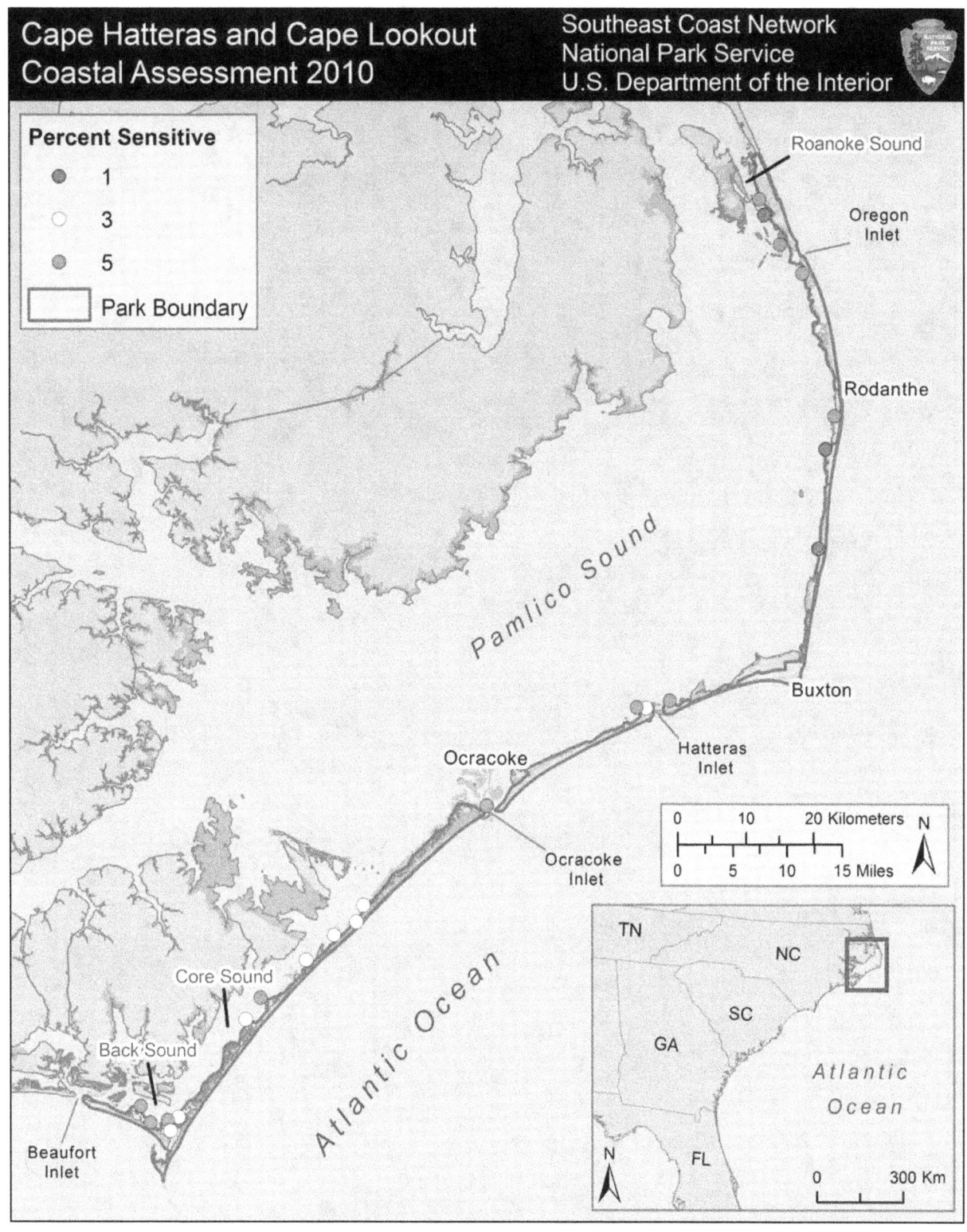

Figure 7. Component scores for the sensitive taxa metric of the Southeast Coast Benthic Index based on samples collected at Cape Hatteras and Cape Lookout National Seashores, 2010. Sites were given scores of 1 (*Poor*), 3 (*Fair*), or 5 (*Good*) based on criteria presented in Table 2 (From Van Dolah et al. 1999).

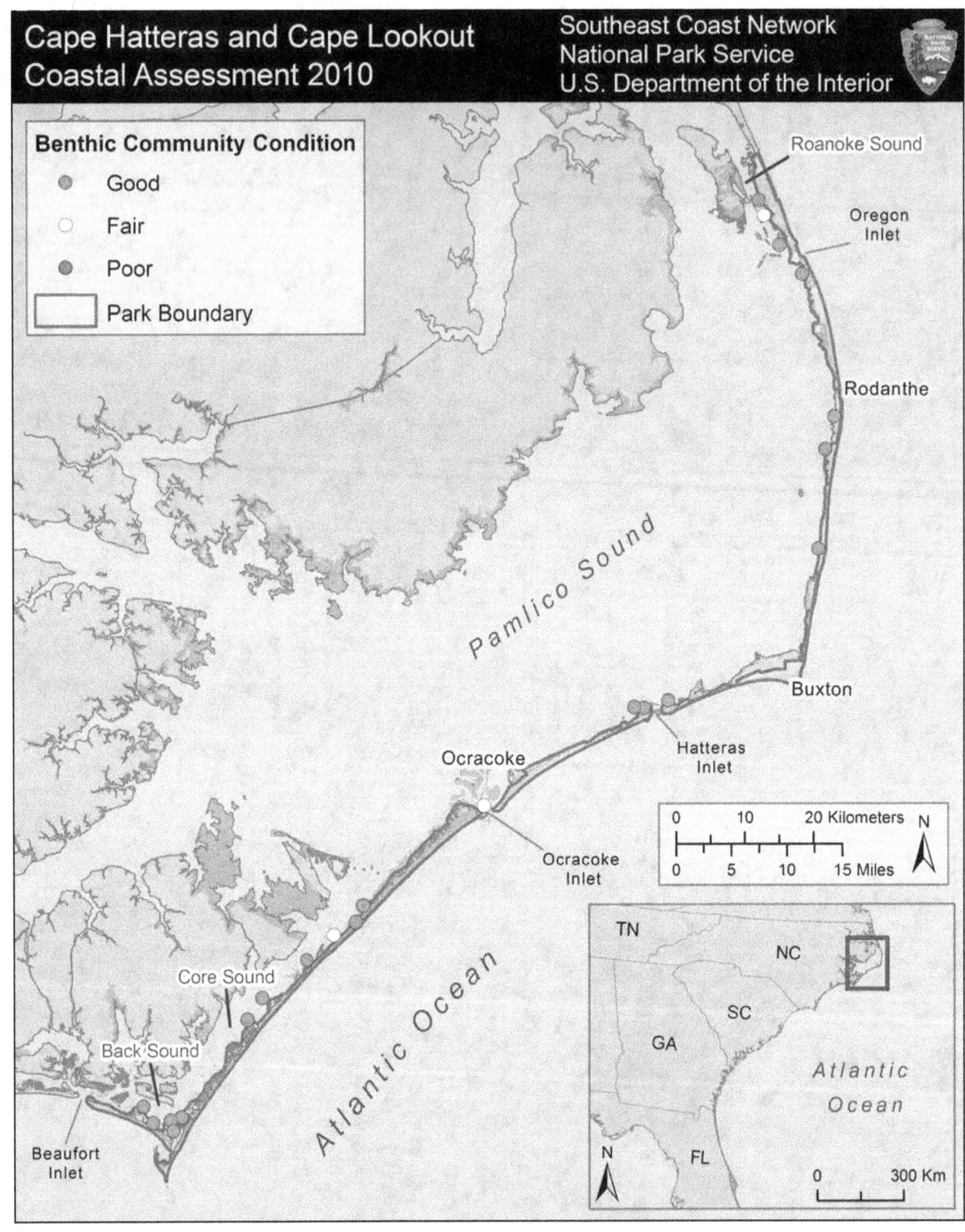

Figure 8. Overall Southeast Coast Benthic Index scores for sites sampled at Cape Hatteras and Cape Lookout National Seashores, 2010. Sites were given assessment ratings of *Good*, *Fair*, or *Poor* based on criteria presented in Table 3 (From Van Dolah et al. 1999).

Literature Cited

DeVivo, J. C., C. J. Wright, M. W. Byrne, E. DiDonato, and T. Curtis. 2008. Vital signs monitoring in the Southeast Coast Inventory & Monitoring Network. Natural Resource Report NPS/SECN/NRR—2008/061. National Park Service, Fort Collins, Colorado.

Gregory M. B., J.C. DeVivo, E. M. DiDonato, C. J. Wright, and E. Thompson. *In Review*. Methods for Monitoring and assessment of estuarine water and sediment quality in Southeast Coast Network Parks. Natural Resource Report NPS/SECN/NRR—2012/xxx. National Park Service, Fort Collins Colorado.

Gregory, M. B., and K. A. Smith. 2011. Assessment of estuarine water and sediment quality at Cape Lookout and Cape Hatteras National Seashores, 2010. Natural Resource Data Series NPS/SECN/NRDS—2011/179. National Park Service, Fort Collins, Colorado.

Holland, A. F., D. M. Sanger, C. P. Gawle, S. B. Lerberg, M. S. Santiago, G. H. M. Riekerk, L. E. Zimmerman, and G. I. Scott. 2004. Linkages between tidal creek ecosystems and the landscape and demographic attributes of their wetlands. Journal of Experimental Marine Biology and Ecology 298: 151-178.

Lerberg, S. B., A. F. Holland, and D. Sanger. 2000. Responses of tidal creek macrobenthic communities to the effects of watershed development. Estuaries 23(6): 838-853.

Mallin, Michael A. V. L. Johnson, and M. R. McIver. 2004. Assessment of Coastal Water Resources and Watershed Conditions in Cape Lookout National Seashore North Carolina. Technical Report NPS/NRWRD/NRTR-2004/322.

North Carolina Department of Environment and Natural Resources (NCDENR). 2001. White Oak River Basinwide Water Quality Plan. North Carolina Department of Environment and Natural Resources, Division of Water Quality, Raleigh, N.C. (A document providing detailed information on land use, demographics, water quality, water body use ratings, and water sampling programs in the New River and White Oak Rivers and their estuaries and watersheds, as well as Back Sound and southern Core Sounds).

North Carolina Department of Environment and Natural Resources Division of Environmental Health-Shellfish Sanitation and Recreational Water Quality Section (NCDENR DEH-SSRWQ). 2011. GIS Coverage for shellfish areas (online at http://data.nconemap.com/geoportal/catalog/search/resource/details.page?uuid=%7B68375E FD-5AF4-4656-B65C-A266913B9F28%7D)

Stevens, D. L., Jr. 1997. Variable density grid-based sampling designs for continuous spatial populations. Envirometrics 8: 167-195.

Stevens, D. L., Jr. and A. R. Olsen. 1999. Spatially restricted surveys over time for aquatic resources. Journal of Agricultural, Biological and Environmental Statistics 4: 415-428.

Stevens, D. and A. R. Olsen. 2004. Spatially balanced sampling of natural resources. Journal of the American Statistical Association 99: 262-278.

U.S. Census Bureau. 2001. GIS coverage of urban areas U.S. Census Bureau U.S. Department of Commerce, U.S. Census Bureau, Washington, DC. (Available at: http://www.census.gov/main/www/cen2000.html).

U.S. EPA. 1995. Environmental Monitoring and Assessment Program (EMAP): Laboratory Methods Manual-Estuaries, Volume 1: Biological and Physical Analyses. U.S. Environmental Protection Agency, Office of Research and Development, Narragansett, RI. EPA/620/R-95/008.

U.S. EPA. 2001. Environmental Monitoring and Assessment Program (EMAP). National Coastal Assessment Quality Assurance Project Plan 2001 – 2004. United States Environmental Protection Agency, Office of Research and Development, National Health and Environmental Effects Research Laboratory, Gulf Ecology Division, Gulf Breeze, FL. EPA/620/R-01/002.

U.S. EPA. 2010. National Coastal Assessment: Field Operations Manual. U. S. Environmental Protection Agency, Office of Research and Development, National Health and Environmental Effects Research Laboratory, Gulf Ecology Division, Gulf Breeze, FL. EPA 620/R-01/003. pp72.

U.S. EPA. 2011. 303-d listed water bodies (GIS Coverage) US EPA Office of Water. (Database and coverage available online at http://www.epa.gov/waters/data/downloads.html#303(d) Listed Impaired Waters.

U. S. Fish and Wildlife Service. 2011. National Wetlands Inventory website. U.S. Department of the Interior, Fish and Wildlife Service, Washington, D.C. (available online at http://www.fws.gov/wetlands/)

Van Dolah, R. F., J. L. Hyland, A. F. Holland, J. S. Rosen, and T. R. Snoots. 1999. A benthic index of biological integrity for assessing habitat quality in estuaries of the southeastern USA. Marine Environmental Research 48: 269-283.

Appendix A. Species Identification Data

Table A-1. Number of individuals observed per taxon during marine benthic macroinvertebrate surveys conducted at Cape Hatteras and Cape Lookout Nations Seashores, July, 2010. See Figure 3 for a map of sample locations.

	Taxon	1	2	4	6	8	10	12	17	20	21	26	A02	A03	A05	A06	A07	A10	A12	A17	A19	A27	A28
Gastropoda	Acteocina canaliculata	3	0	11	0	0	1	46	0	27	12	0	7	0	0	0	8	12	35	4	0	2	27
	Calyptraeidae	0	0	0	1	0	0	0	0	0	0	0	0	0	0	0	0	0	0	0	0	0	0
	Cerithiopsis sp.	0	0	0	0	0	0	0	0	0	0	0	0	0	0	0	0	0	0	0	0	0	0
	Gastropoda	0	0	0	2	0	0	0	0	4	0	1	0	0	0	0	0	1	0	0	0	0	0
	Haminoea solitaria	0	0	7	0	0	3	2	0	8	0	2	0	0	0	0	1	1	0	0	0	6	0
	Hydrobiidae	0	0	0	0	0	0	0	0	0	0	0	0	0	0	0	0	0	0	0	0	4	0
	Ilyanassa obsoleta	0	0	4	0	0	0	3	0	0	0	0	0	0	0	0	0	0	0	0	0	0	0
	Nassarius acutus	0	0	0	0	0	0	0	0	0	0	0	1	0	0	0	0	0	0	0	0	0	0
	Odostomia sp.	0	0	0	0	0	0	0	0	0	0	0	0	0	0	0	0	0	0	0	0	1	0
	Olivella mutica	0	0	0	0	2	0	0	0	0	0	0	0	0	0	0	0	0	0	0	0	0	0
	Pyramidella crenulata	0	0	3	0	0	0	0	0	0	0	0	0	0	0	0	0	0	0	0	0	0	0
	Rictaxis punctostriatus	0	0	0	0	0	2	1	0	0	0	0	0	0	0	0	0	1	0	1	0	1	2
	Turbonilla sp.	0	0	0	0	0	0	0	0	0	0	0	7	0	0	0	0	0	0	0	0	0	0
Bivalvia	Bivalvia	0	0	0	2	2	0	0	15	0	4	0	0	0	0	0	2	0	0	0	0	0	0
	Caryocorbula caribaea	0	0	0	0	0	0	0	0	0	0	0	4	0	0	0	0	0	0	0	0	0	0
	Donax variabilis	0	2	0	0	0	0	0	0	0	0	0	0	0	0	0	0	0	0	0	0	0	0
	Ennucula sp.	0	0	1	0	0	0	0	0	1	0	0	6	0	0	0	0	0	0	0	0	0	0
	Ensis minor	0	0	0	0	0	0	0	1	1	1	0	0	0	0	0	0	0	0	0	0	0	0
	Gemma gemma	0	1	9	0	8	0	16	0	0	8	0	0	0	0	0	10	12	800	2,796	0	27	53
	Lucinoma filosa	0	0	0	0	0	6	0	0	0	0	0	2	0	0	0	0	0	0	0	0	0	0
	Macoma tenta	0	0	0	0	0	0	0	0	0	0	0	0	0	0	0	0	0	0	0	0	24	0
	Mulinia lateralis	0	0	0	0	0	0	0	0	0	0	0	1	0	0	0	0	0	0	0	0	0	0
	Musculus lateralis	0	0	0	0	3	0	0	0	0	0	0	0	0	0	0	0	0	0	0	0	0	0
	Parvilucina multilineata	1	0	1	0	0	0	1	0	6	0	0	0	0	0	0	0	0	1	0	0	4	0
	Solemya velum	0	0	1	0	0	0	1	0	1	0	0	0	0	0	0	0	0	0	0	0	0	0
	Spisula solidissima	0	2	0	0	1	0	0	0	0	0	0	0	0	0	0	0	0	0	0	0	0	0
	Tellina iris	0	0	0	0	0	0	0	0	2	0	0	0	0	0	0	0	0	0	0	0	0	0
	Tellina sp.	0	0	2	0	11	117	2	3	0	0	1	2	2	0	3	0	3	0	0	0	0	0

Taxon		1	2	4	6	8	10	12	17	20	21	26	A02	A03	A05	A06	A07	A10	A12	A17	A19	A27	A28
	Tellina versicolor	0	0	0	0	0	0	0	0	0	0	0	2	0	0	0	0	0	0	0	0	0	1
	Tellinidae	2	0	0	0	0	0	0	0	0	0	0	0	4	0	0	0	0	0	0	0	0	0
Crustacea	*Acanthohaustorius* sp.	0	0	0	0	0	0	0	23	0	0	0	0	0	0	0	9	0	0	0	0	0	0
	Amakusanthura magnifica	0	0	0	0	3	0	0	0	0	0	0	0	0	0	11	0	0	0	0	0	0	0
	Ameroculodes sp.	0	0	0	0	0	0	1	0	0	0	0	0	0	0	0	0	0	0	0	0	0	0
	Ampelisca sp.	0	0	0	0	0	1	0	0	0	0	0	0	0	0	0	0	0	0	0	0	0	0
	Ampelisca verrilli	0	0	0	0	0	0	10	0	3	0	0	6	0	0	0	0	1	0	2	0	0	0
	Amphipoda	0	0	0	1	0	0	0	0	0	0	0	0	0	0	0	0	0	0	0	0	0	0
	Ampithoidae	0	0	0	0	0	0	0	0	0	1	0	0	0	1	0	0	0	0	0	0	3	0
	Ancinus depressus	0	0	0	0	0	0	0	0	0	1	0	0	0	1	0	0	0	0	0	0	0	0
	Balanus amphitrite	0	0	0	0	0	0	0	0	0	0	0	0	0	0	5	0	0	0	0	0	0	0
	Batea catharinensis	0	0	0	0	10	0	0	0	0	0	0	0	0	0	0	0	0	0	0	0	0	0
	Bathyporeia parkeri	0	0	0	0	0	0	0	0	1	0	0	0	0	1	0	0	0	0	0	0	0	0
	Bowmaniella dissimilis	0	0	0	0	0	2	0	0	0	0	0	0	0	0	0	0	0	0	0	0	0	0
	Caprella geometrica	0	0	0	0	17	0	0	0	0	0	0	0	0	0	2	0	0	0	0	0	0	0
	Chiridotea arenicola	0	15	0	0	0	0	0	4	0	0	0	0	0	0	0	0	0	0	0	0	0	0
	Edotea montosa	1	0	0	0	0	0	0	0	0	0	0	0	0	0	0	0	0	0	0	0	1	0
	Elasmopus levis	0	0	0	0	6	0	0	0	0	0	0	0	0	0	0	0	0	0	0	0	0	0
	Erichsonella sp.	0	0	0	0	2	0	0	0	0	0	0	0	2	0	0	0	0	0	0	0	0	0
	Ericthonius brasiliensis	0	0	0	0	2	0	0	0	0	0	0	0	0	0	0	0	0	0	0	0	0	0
	Gammarus mucronatus	0	0	0	0	0	0	0	0	0	5	0	0	0	0	0	0	0	0	0	0	2	0
	Haustoriidae	0	0	0	0	0	0	0	0	0	0	0	0	0	3	0	0	0	0	1	0	0	0
	Lembos smithi	0	0	0	0	5	0	0	0	0	0	0	0	0	0	0	0	0	0	0	0	0	0
	Lepidactylus dytiscus	0	0	0	0	2	0	0	0	0	0	0	0	2	0	0	0	0	0	0	0	0	0
	Leptocheliidae	0	0	0	0	2	0	0	0	0	0	0	0	0	0	0	1	0	0	0	0	0	0
	Leucon americanus	0	0	0	0	0	0	0	0	0	0	0	1	0	0	0	0	0	0	0	0	1	0
	Listriella barnardi	0	0	2	0	1	0	3	0	0	0	0	1	1	0	0	0	0	0	0	0	0	0
	Listriella clymenellae	0	0	0	0	0	0	0	0	0	0	0	5	0	0	0	0	0	0	0	0	0	0
	Lysianopsis alba	0	0	0	0	4	0	0	0	0	0	0	0	0	0	0	0	0	0	0	0	0	0

Table A-1. Continued.

Taxon		1	2	4	6	8	10	12	17	20	21	26	A02	A03	A05	A06	A07	A10	A12	A17	A19	A27	A28
	Monocorophium acherusicum	0	0	0	0	2	0	0	0	0	0	0	0	0	0	0	0	0	0	0	0	0	0
	Oedicerotidae	0	0	0	0	0	0	0	0	0	0	0	0	0	1	0	0	0	0	0	0	0	0
	Ostracoda	0	0	11	1	17	5	1	0	4	5	0	4	0	0	0	2	2	14	9	0	68	2
	Oxyurostylis smithi	0	0	0	0	0	1	0	0	0	0	0	1	0	0	0	0	1	0	0	0	0	0
	Paracaprella tenuis	0	0	0	0	5	0	0	0	0	0	0	0	0	0	2	0	0	0	0	0	0	0
	Parahaustorius longimerus	0	2	0	0	0	0	0	26	0	0	0	0	0	0	0	0	0	0	0	0	0	0
	Paraphoxus spinosus	0	0	0	0	3	0	0	0	0	0	0	0	0	0	0	0	0	0	0	0	0	0
	Pinnotheridae	0	0	0	0	0	0	0	0	0	0	0	2	0	0	0	0	0	0	0	0	0	0
	Protohaustorius bousfieldi	0	0	0	0	0	0	0	0	0	0	0	0	0	0	3	0	0	0	0	0	0	0
	Protohaustorius deichmannae	0	0	0	0	7	0	0	0	0	0	0	0	0	0	0	0	0	0	0	0	0	0
	Rudilemboides naglei	0	0	0	0	15	0	0	0	0	0	0	0	0	0	0	0	0	0	0	0	0	0
	Spilocuma watlingi	0	0	0	0	0	0	0	0	0	0	0	0	0	0	1	0	0	0	0	0	0	0
	Stenothoe minuta	0	0	0	0	8	0	0	0	0	0	0	0	0	0	0	0	0	0	0	0	0	0
	Synchelidium americanum	0	0	0	0	4	0	0	0	0	0	0	0	0	0	0	0	0	0	0	0	0	0
	Trichophoxus epistomus	0	0	9	0	25	0	0	0	11	0	0	0	0	0	15	1	0	0	0	0	0	3
Annelida	Oligochaeta	1	0	0	2	0	3	24	0	1	0	15	0	0	0	0	0	0	0	0	0	0	0
Polychaeta	*Aglaophamus verrilli*	0	0	0	0	0	0	0	0	0	0	0	2	0	0	0	0	0	0	0	0	0	0
	Armandia agilis	0	0	0	0	0	0	0	0	0	0	1	0	0	0	0	0	0	0	0	0	0	0
	Armandia maculata	0	0	0	0	6	0	0	0	0	0	0	0	0	0	2	0	0	0	0	0	0	0
	Asabellides oculata	0	0	0	0	0	1	1	0	0	0	0	0	0	0	0	0	0	0	0	0	0	0
	Brania wellfleetensis	0	0	0	0	0	1	0	0	0	0	0	0	0	0	1	0	0	0	1	0	0	0
	Capitella capitata	1	0	0	0	0	0	0	0	0	0	0	0	0	0	0	0	0	0	0	0	1	0
	Capitella jonesi	0	0	1	0	0	1	0	0	0	0	0	0	0	0	0	0	0	1	0	0	6	0
	Ceratonereis irritabilis	0	0	1	0	0	0	0	0	0	0	0	0	0	0	0	0	0	0	0	1	0	0
	Cirratulidae	0	0	0	0	0	0	1	0	0	0	0	0	0	0	0	5	0	0	0	0	0	0
	Clymenella mucosa	0	0	0	0	21	0	0	0	0	0	0	3	0	0	1	0	0	0	0	0	0	0
	Clymenella torquata	0	0	0	0	0	0	0	0	0	0	0	4	0	0	0	0	0	0	0	0	0	0

Table A-1. Continued.

Taxon	1	2	4	6	8	10	12	17	20	21	26	A02	A03	A05	A06	A07	A10	A12	A17	A19	A27	A28
Clymenella zonalis	0	0	0	0	0	0	0	0	0	0	0	2	0	0	0	0	0	0	0	0	0	0
Dipolydora cardalia	0	0	0	0	0	0	1	0	0	0	1	0	0	0	0	0	0	0	0	0	0	0
Dipolydora socialis	0	0	0	0	2	0	0	0	0	0	0	0	0	0	0	0	0	0	0	0	0	0
Enoplobranchus sanguineus	0	0	1	0	0	0	0	0	0	0	0	0	0	0	0	0	0	1	0	0	0	0
Eteone foliosa	0	0	0	2	0	1	0	0	0	0	0	0	0	0	0	2	0	2	0	0	0	0
Eumida sanguinea	0	0	0	0	1	0	0	0	0	0	0	0	0	0	0	0	0	0	0	0	0	0
Exogone dispar	0	0	0	0	1	0	0	0	0	0	0	0	0	0	0	0	0	0	0	0	0	0
Glycera oxycephala	6	0	3	0	0	0	0	0	0	0	1	2	0	0	0	0	0	0	0	0	0	0
Glycera sp.	0	0	0	0	0	0	0	0	4	0	0	0	0	0	1	0	0	0	0	0	0	0
Glycinde solitaria	0	0	0	0	0	2	0	0	0	1	0	2	0	0	0	0	1	4	0	0	5	2
Glycinde sp.	0	0	0	1	0	0	0	0	0	0	0	0	0	0	0	0	0	0	0	0	0	0
Heteromastus filiformis	2	0	0	5	0	0	0	0	0	1	1	0	0	0	0	2	0	2	0	0	0	0
Hypereteone heteropoda	0	0	0	13	0	0	0	0	0	2	0	0	1	0	0	1	0	0	1	0	0	0
Kinbergonuphis sp.	0	0	0	0	0	0	0	0	0	0	0	0	0	0	0	0	1	0	0	0	0	0
Leitoscoloplos fragilis	0	0	5	0	6	4	3	0	1	1	7	0	3	0	0	0	2	2	0	8	2	7
Magelona riojai	0	0	0	0	0	0	0	0	0	0	0	1	0	0	1	0	0	0	0	0	0	0
Maldanidae	0	0	0	0	0	0	0	0	0	0	0	1	0	0	0	0	0	0	0	0	0	0
Marenzellaria viridis	3	0	0	9	0	0	0	1	0	0	0	0	0	0	0	3	0	1	0	11	0	0
Mediomastus ambiseta	18	0	0	0	0	15	0	0	0	0	13	0	10	0	0	0	0	0	0	0	0	0
Mediomastus sp.	0	0	0	0	0	0	0	0	1	0	0	0	0	0	0	0	0	1	0	2	0	0
Microphthalmus sczelkowii	0	0	0	0	0	0	0	0	0	0	0	0	0	1	0	0	0	0	0	0	0	0
Neanthes arenaceodentata	0	0	1	0	3	0	0	0	0	0	1	0	0	0	2	0	0	1	0	0	0	0
Nephtys picta	0	0	0	0	0	3	0	0	0	0	0	0	0	0	4	0	1	0	0	0	0	0
Nereididae	0	0	0	0	0	0	0	0	0	0	0	0	0	0	0	0	0	3	0	0	0	0
Nereis lamellosa	0	0	0	0	0	0	0	0	0	0	0	0	0	0	0	0	0	0	0	0	0	0
Notomastus latericeus	0	0	0	0	1	0	0	0	0	0	0	8	0	0	0	0	1	0	0	0	0	0
Ophelina sp.	0	0	0	0	1	0	0	0	1	0	0	0	0	0	0	0	0	0	0	0	0	0
Owenia fusiformis	0	0	0	0	0	1	0	0	0	0	0	2	0	0	0	0	0	0	0	0	0	0

Table A-1. Continued.

Taxon		1	2	4	6	8	10	12	17	20	21	26	A02	A03	A05	A06	A07	A10	A12	A17	A19	A27	A28
	Paradoneis lyra	0	0	0	0	0	0	0	0	0	0	0	0	0	0	1	0	0	0	0	0	0	0
	Paraonis fulgens	0	5	0	0	6	0	2	1	0	0	0	0	0	16	4	0	0	0	1	0	0	0
	Paraprionospio sp.	0	0	0	0	0	2	0	0	0	0	1	6	0	0	0	0	0	0	0	0	0	0
	Phyllodoce mucosa	0	0	0	0	1	0	0	0	0	0	0	4	0	0	0	0	0	0	0	0	0	0
	Platynereis dumerilii	0	0	0	0	2	0	0	0	0	0	0	0	0	0	0	0	0	0	0	0	1	0
	Podarke obscura	0	0	0	0	1	0	0	0	0	0	0	0	0	0	0	1	0	0	0	0	0	0
	Podarkeopsis levifuscina	0	0	0	0	0	0	0	0	0	0	0	0	0	0	0	0	1	0	0	0	0	0
	Polydora sp.	0	1	0	0	1	0	0	0	0	0	0	0	0	0	0	0	0	0	0	0	0	0
	Prionospio heterobranchia	0	0	5	20	0	0	14	0	0	6	4	0	0	0	0	5	0	17	0	0	7	0
	Prionospio pygmaeus	4	0	0	0	0	23	0	0	6	0	0	0	0	0	0	0	0	0	0	0	5	0
	Prionospio sp.	0	0	0	0	1	0	0	0	0	0	2	0	0	0	0	0	0	0	1	0	0	0
	Sabellaria floridensis	0	0	0	0	1	0	0	0	0	0	0	0	0	0	0	0	0	0	0	0	0	0
	Salvatoria clavata	0	0	0	2	4	8	0	0	0	0	16	0	0	0	0	3	0	3	0	0	0	0
	Scolelepis texana	0	0	1	13	0	0	3	0	0	11	1	0	0	0	0	4	0	0	2	0	1	0
	Scoloplos rubra	0	0	0	0	0	0	0	0	0	0	0	0	0	0	0	0	0	0	1	0	0	0
	Sphaerosyllis longicauda	0	0	0	0	1	0	0	0	0	0	0	0	0	0	0	0	0	0	0	0	0	0
	Spio pettiboneae	0	0	0	0	0	6	0	0	0	0	2	0	0	0	1	0	0	0	0	0	0	0
	Spiophanes bombyx	0	0	0	0	2	9	0	1	0	0	0	1	0	0	0	0	0	0	0	12	1	1
	Streblospio benedicti	6	1	0	0	0	0	0	1	0	1	2	0	10	0	0	0	0	0	0	0	0	0
	Syllis sp.	0	0	0	0	0	0	0	0	0	0	0	0	0	0	0	0	0	1	0	0	0	0
	Tharyx acutus	0	0	0	0	0	0	0	0	0	0	8	0	0	0	0	0	1	0	0	0	0	0
	Tharyx sp. A sensu MWRA, 2007	12	0	34	0	0	0	0	0	0	0	1	0	0	0	0	0	1	0	10	0	2	2
Echinodermata	Echinoidea	0	0	0	0	0	0	0	1	0	0	0	0	0	0	0	0	0	0	0	0	0	0
	Holothuroidea	0	0	0	6	0	3	0	0	0	0	0	0	0	0	0	5	0	0	0	0	0	0
	Leptosynapta inhaerens	0	0	0	0	2	0	2	0	0	0	0	0	0	0	0	0	0	0	0	0	0	0
Nemertea	*Amphiporus* sp.	0	0	0	0	0	0	0	0	0	1	0	0	0	0	0	0	0	0	0	0	0	0
	Carinoma tremaphoros	0	0	1	0	0	0	0	0	0	0	0	0	0	0	0	0	0	0	0	0	0	0
	Carinomella lactea	0	0	0	0	0	1	0	0	0	0	1	2	0	0	0	0	0	0	0	0	0	0
	Micrura sp.	0	0	0	0	0	1	0	0	0	0	0	0	0	0	1	0	0	0	0	0	0	0

Table A-1. Continued.

Taxon		1	2	4	6	8	10	12	17	20	21	26	A02	A03	A05	A06	A07	A10	A12	A17	A19	A27	A28
	Nemertea	0	0	0	0	0	0	0	0	0	0	0	0	0	0	1	0	0	0	0	0	0	0
	Tetrastemma sp.	0	0	0	0	0	0	0	0	0	1	0	0	0	0	0	0	0	0	0	0	0	0
Brachiopoda	*Glottidia pyramidata*	0	0	0	0	0	1	0	0	0	0	0	0	0	0	0	0	0	0	0	0	0	0
Phoronida	*Phoronis psammophila*	0	0	0	2	0	2	2	0	0	2	0	0	0	0	0	0	0	0	0	0	0	0
Cephalochordata	*Branchiostoma* sp.	0	0	0	0	0	0	0	0	0	0	0	0	0	0	2	0	0	0	0	0	0	0
Other Organisms	Actiniaria	0	0	0	0	0	2	0	0	0	0	0	0	0	0	0	0	0	0	0	0	0	0
	Nematoda	0	0	0	0	0	0	0	0	0	0	0	0	0	0	0	0	0	0	0	0	1	0
TOTAL		60	29	114	83	228	227	140	77	83	63	81	91	31	24	64	65	42	882	2,838	35	176	100

Appendix B. Taxonomic Quality Control Assessment

ECOANALYSTS, INC.
LIFE IN WATER

EcoAnalysts, Inc.
1420 South Blaine Street, Suite 14
Moscow, Idaho 83843 U.S.A.
(208) 882-2588

National Park Service
5806: NPS GA Marine Benthos 2011

Taxonomy ID QC Percent Similarity

Report Count: 4

5806.1-5
Component: General

Site ID	Container #	Depth (ft.)	Collector
CAHACAL008	5	4.6	B. Gregory

Comparison Date: 02/09/2012 02:34:40

TIN	TAXON	NOTE	Original Taxonomist - Matthew Hill				QC Taxonomist - John Pfeiffer				NOTE	DIFF.
			AB	L	P	A	AB	L	P	A		
6667	Amakusanthura magnifica		2	2	0	0	2	2	0	0		0
3938	Ampelisca		0	0	0	0	0	0	0	0		0
6737	Batea catharinensis		9	9	0	0	9	9	0	0		0
8476	Caprella geometrica		16	16	0	0	18	18	0	0		-2
6571	Elasmopus levis		5	5	0	0	5	5	0	0		0
6294	Erichsonella		0	0	0	0	0	0	0	0		0
6937	Ericthonius brasiliensis		0	0	0	0	0	0	0	0		0
6120	Gemma gemma		8	8	0	0	8	8	0	0		0
6633	Lembos smithi		4	4	0	0	4	4	0	0		0
3937	Leptochelidae	remarks	2	2	0	0	2	2	0	0		0
8478	Leptosynapta inhaerens		0	0	0	0	0	0	0	0		0
6596	Listriella barnardi		1	1	0	0	1	1	0	0		0
6070	Lysianopsis alba		3	3	0	0	1	1	0	0		2
6463	Monocorophium acherusicum		0	0	0	0	0	0	0	0		0
7162	Musculus lateralis		2	2	0	0	2	2	0	0		0
6285	Olivella mutica		1	1	0	0	1	1	0	0		0
121	Ostracoda		17	17	0	0	12	12	0	0		5
6561	Paracaprella tenuis		4	4	0	0	4	4	0	0		0
7494	Paraphoxus spinosus		2	2	0	0	2	2	0	0		0
8475	Protohaustorius deichmannae		6	6	0	0	6	6	0	0		0
7359	Rudilemboides naglei		14	14	0	0	14	14	0	0	.	0

EcoAnalysts, Inc.
1420 South Blaine Street, Suite 14
Moscow, Idaho 83843 U.S.A.
(208) 882 - 2588

National Park Service
5806: NPS GA Marine Benthos 2011

EcoANALYSTS, INC.

Taxonomy ID QC Percent Similarity

5806.1-5

Report Count: 4

Component: General

Comparison Date: 02/09/2012 02:34:40
(Cont'd.)

Site ID	Container #	Depth (ft.)	Collector
CAHACAL008	5	4.6	B. Gregory

		Original Taxonomist - Matthew Hill					QC Taxonomist - John Pfeiffer					
TIN	TAXON	AB	L	P	A	NOTE	AB	L	P	A	NOTE	DIFF.
7404	Spisula solidissima	1	1	0	0		1	1	0	0		0
6043	Stenothoe minuta	7	7	0	0		7	7	0	0		0
8477	Synchelidium americanum	3	3	0	0		3	3	0	0		0
4021	Tellina	11	11	0	0		11	11	0	0		0
6964	Trichophoxus epistomus	25	25	0	0		20	20	0	0		5
		143					133					

Difference = 10
Percent Similarity = 93.34

EcoAnalysts, Inc.
1420 South Blaine Street, Suite 14
Moscow, Idaho 83843 U.S.A.
(208) 882 - 2589

ECOANALYSTS, INC.
LIFE IN WATER

Taxonomy ID QC Percent Similarity

5806.1-5
Component: Annelids

Comparison Date: 02/07/2012 02:17:41

Site ID	Container #	Depth (ft.)	Collector
CAHACAL008	5	4.6	B. Gregory

			Original Taxonomist - Chip Barrett				QC Taxonomist - Matthew Hill					
TIN	TAXON	NOTE	AB	L	P	A	AB	L	P	A	NOTE	DIFF.
8473	Amandia maculata		5	5	0	0	5	5	0	0		0
6383	Clymenella mucosa		20	20	0	0	20	20	0	0		0
6389	Dipolydora socialis		1	1	0	0	1	1	0	0		0
6302	Eumida sanguinea		0	0	0	0	0	0	0	0		0
6392	Exogone dispar		0	0	0	0	0	0	0	0		0
4378	Glycinde multidens		0	0	0	0	0	0	0	0		0
4177	Leitoscoloplos fragilis		7	7	0	0	6	6	0	0		1
6123	Neanthes arenaceodentata		3	3	0	0	3	3	0	0		0
3554	Nereididae	Not acuminata nor cylindricaudata	0	0	0	0	1	1	0	0		-1
7929	Ophelina		1	1	0	0	1	1	0	0		0
6341	Paraonis fulgens		6	6	0	0	6	6	0	0		0
6300	Phyllodoce mucosa		1	1	0	0	1	1	0	0		0
6268	Platynereis dumerilii		1	1	0	0	0	0	0	0		1
6270	Podarke obscura		0	0	0	0	0	0	0	0		0
4185	Polydora		1	1	0	0	1	1	0	0		0
6338	Prionospio	Probably P. heterobranchia	0	0	0	0	0	0	0	0		0
7671	Sabellaria floridensis		0	0	0	0	0	0	0	0		0
6379	Salvatoria clavata		4	4	0	0	4	4	0	0		0
6364	Sphaerosyllis longicauda		0	0	0	0	0	0	0	0		0
5838	Spiophanes bombyx Complex		2	2	0	0	2	2	0	0		0

EcoAnalysts, Inc.
1420 South Blaine Street, Suite 14
Moscow, Idaho 83843 U.S.A.
(208) 882 - 2588

ECOANALYSTS, INC.
LIFE IN WATER

Taxonomy ID QC Percent Similarity

52	51

Difference =	1
Percent Similarity =	96.38

EcoAnalysts, Inc.
1420 South Blaine Street, Suite 14
Moscow, Idaho 83843 U.S.A.
(208) 892-2588

Taxonomy ID QC Percent Similarity

5806.1-11
Component: General

Comparison Date: 02/09/2012 12:59:36

Site ID	Container #	Depth (ft.)	Collector
CAHACAL026	11/12	3	B. Gregory

			Original Taxonomist - Matthew Hill				QC Taxonomist - John Pfeiffer					
TIN	TAXON	NOTE	AB	L	P	A	AB	L	P	A	NOTE	DIFF.
6801	Carinomella lactea		1	1	0	0	1	1	0	0		0
4174	Haminoea solitaria		2	2	0	0	2	2	0	0		0
4021	Tellina		1	1	0	0	1	1	0	0		0
			4				4					0

Difference = 0

Percent Similarity = 100.00

EcoAnalysts, Inc.
1420 South Blaine Street, Suite 14
Moscow, Idaho 83843 U.S.A.
(208) 882-2588

ECO ANALYSTS, INC.
LIFE IN WATER

Taxonomy ID QC Percent Similarity

5806.1-11
Component: Annelids

Comparison Date: 02/07/2012 02:17:23

Site ID	Container #	Depth (ft.)	Collector
CAHACAL026	11/12	3	B. Gregory

TIN	TAXON	NOTE	Original Taxonomist - Chip Barrett				QC Taxonomist - Matthew Hill				NOTE	DIFF.
			AB	L	P	A	AB	L	P	A		
7619	Armandia agilis		0	0	0	0	0	0	0	0		0
7995	Dipolydora cardalia		0	0	0	0	0	0	0	0		0
8470	Glycera oxycephala		1	1	0	0	1	1	0	0		0
4380	Heteromastus filiformis		1	1	0	0	1	1	0	0		0
4177	Leitoscoloplos fragilis		7	7	0	0	7	7	0	0		0
6018	Mediomastus ambiseta		13	13	0	0	13	13	0	0		0
6123	Neanthes arenaceodentata		1	1	0	0	1	1	0	0		0
5982	Paraprionospio		0	0	0	0	1	1	0	0		-1
4391	Paraprionospio pinnata		1	1	0	0	0	0	0	0		1
6338	Prionospio	Probably P. pygmaeus	2	2	0	0	2	2	0	0		0
6339	Prionospio heterobranchia		4	4	0	0	4	4	0	0		0
6379	Salvatoria clavata		16	16	0	0	16	16	0	0		0
6129	Scolelepis texana		1	1	0	0	1	1	0	0		0
7698	Spio pettiboneae		1	1	0	0	1	1	0	0		0
4043	Streblospio benedicti		2	2	0	0	2	2	0	0		0
4186	Tharyx acutus		7	7	0	0	7	7	0	0		0
7489	Tharyx sp. A sensu MWRA, 2007		0	0	0	0	0	0	0	0		0
			57				57					

Difference = 0
Percent Similarity = 98.25

www.ingramcontent.com/pod-product-compliance
Lightning Source LLC
Chambersburg PA
CBHW080924290526
45795CB00007BA/2640